Railways & Recollectio

Contents

© David Phillips 2014
Photographs © The NOSTALGIA Collection archive

First published in 2014

British Library Cataloguing in Publication Data
A catalogue record for this book is available from the British Library.

ISBN 978 1 85794 402 0

Silver Link Publishing Ltd
The Trundle
Ringstead Road
Great Addington
Kettering
Northants NN14 4BW

Tel/Fax: 01536 330588
email: sales@nostalgiacollection.com
Website: www.nostalgiacollection.com

Printed and bound in the Czech Republic

Front cover: **MACHYNLLETH** Just in case you're wondering why all the passengers on the platform have their backs turned to the trains, it's probably because the station commands a splendid view across the stunning Dyfi estuary. Machynlleth station was built by the Newtown & Machynlleth Railway, and today is a vital lifeline to Aberystwyth and the Cambrian coast to the west, and to Newtown and Shrewsbury to the east.

Frontispiece: **BARMOUTH** It's 25 May 1970 and diesel multiple units (DMUs) dominate branch-line Britain – particularly in rural areas, like much of Wales. Nationalised British Rail hoped that replacing expensive steam power with more affordable diesel traction on the less heavily frequented routes would make them profitable, but the nation's railways were still in decline.

Introduction

It's 1970 and the Swinging Sixties are most definitely over. The Beatles are on the brink of splitting up and Harold Wilson's Labour Government, which had been in power for most of the decade, is about to make way for Edward Heath's Conservatives. Eighteen-year-olds now get the vote and the half-crown coin (worth $12\frac{1}{2}$p) is no longer legal tender.

Less than two years earlier, British Rail had consigned to the scrapyard the last of its standard-gauge steam locomotives, despite many of them having decades of useful life left in them.

Electric traction will power the railways of the future, but right now the country cannot afford a wholesale switch to electric railways. Instead, there's the usual British compromise – in other words muddle – with a bewildering variety of diesel locomotives introduced in haste to fill the vacuum left by steam. Some of the new diesel locos are virtually obsolete by the time they are introduced, but in 1970 most of them are still wheezing on.

But it is not all doom and gloom. The introduction of DMUs (diesel multiple units) has cut the cost of running services on the nation's rural branch lines and probably saved more of them from following the fate of the lines cruelly closed under the Beeching axe in the preceding decade. The light, airy feel of the new railbuses is popular with passengers, too. We rail enthusiasts sometimes forget that not everybody was in love with the soot and grime of steam…

The real problem for the railways in 1970 was the network's neglect by politicians. Britain's railways had been nationalised back in 1948 with a fanfare of optimism for the future but, as the cold reality of running a crumbling network dawned, the politicians soon realised that British Rail was a poisoned chalice – and a very expensive one, at that. So they concentrated on building lots of fast new roads instead.

Motorways, bypasses and trunk road upgrades ripped through Britain's green and pleasant land, to the detriment of the railways. Cars had become more affordable, fuel was still cheap and the roads were getting better and better. Passengers deserted the railways in droves.

Yet enthusiasts still remained – not least our own Ray Ruffell, whose photographs grace the pages of this book. Ray lived and breathed railways and had been recording the changing scene with his ever-present camera for more than a decade. Through his lens we get to witness the changes as they happen.

Most of Ray's photographs were taken on his native Southern lines, but as ever he travelled further afield during 1970 – notably to Wales for an extended holiday with his family, as well as a short trip to the Midlands. Thus we get to see much of the country's railway scene in 1970 recorded in Ray's trademark gritty black and white images.

The world of railways – indeed the world in general – had changed a lot between 1960 and 1970. How much would it change in the coming decade? Read on and witness those dramatic changes starting to happen…

Southern Electric

WIMBLEDON PARK Driver Harry Boyes poses for Ray Ruffell's camera at Wimbledon Park on 30 April 1970. Harry is at the controls of venerable 2-BIL No 2062. The former Southern Railway gave the designation 2-BIL to the DC third-rail electric multiple units (EMUs) introduced in the 1930s to run from London Waterloo to the South Coast. and they were so named because each set of two cars had two lavatories (BI-Lavatory), one in each car.

A total of 152 sets were built at Eastleigh and Lancing between 1935 and 1938. They boasted a steel chassis but wooden upper framing, clad in steel panels. The top speed was 60mph. By 1970 most of them had reached the end of the line and were destined for the scrapyard, although one set is preserved at the National Railway Museum in York.

Left: **WIMBLEDON PARK** Here's a close-up of the front end of another 2-BIL, No 2136, at Wimbledon Park on 11 April.

Above: **WIMBLEDON PARK** De-icing units Nos 015 and 019 stand in the sidings on the same day.

Left: **WIMBLEDON PARK** This is Class 418 No 5617. These EMUs were in service from the late 1950s but were designated 2-SAP from 1970 onwards by declassifying the 1st Class accommodation in 2-HAP units. They were used mainly on suburban routes around London.

Below: **WANDSWORTH** It's 29 April and here is a classic view of an eight-car Waterloo-Reading service, headed by No 2692, passing Point Pleasant at Wandsworth.

Left: **WATERLOO** On 5 October 1970 4-COR (4-car CORridor) EMUs Nos 3158 and 3142 approach Waterloo. The corridor connections provided throughout these sets gave them their characteristic front end. Built from 1937 by the Southern Railway, they remained in service with British Rail as Class 404s until 1972.

Below: A brace of 4-CORs stands at Ascot on 5 November – No 3137 on the down line (left) and No 3155 on the up. These EMUs were capable of 75mph.

1970 Happenings

January
- Age of majority in the UK is reduced from 21 to 18.
- Half-crown coin ceases to be legal tender.
- First Boeing 747 Jumbo jet lands at Heathrow Airport.

February
- Hillman Avenger is launched.
- Prince Charles joins the Royal Navy.

March
- Martin Peters becomes England's first £200,000 footballer when he is transferred from West Ham to Tottenham Hotspur.
- Dana wins the Eurovision Song Contest for Ireland with *All Kinds of Everything*.

April
- Everton wins the First Division title.
- Paul McCartney announces that he is leaving the Beatles.
- Chelsea beats Leeds 2-1 in the FA Cup replay after drawing 2-2 in the final.

May
- The Britannia railway bridge across the Menai Strait is badly damaged by fire.
- England football captain Bobby Moore is arrested on suspicion of stealing a bracelet in Bogota, Columbia, on the eve of the 1970 World Cup.

June
- England loses 3-2 to West Germany in the quarter final of the World Cup.
- Edward Heath becomes Prime Minister as the Conservatives win the General Election.

July
- Last issue of grog in the Royal Navy.
- Aswan Dam is completed in Egypt.

August
- Bobby Moore is cleared of stealing the Bogota bracelet.
- Isle of Wight Festival attracts 500,000 music fans.

September
- Guitarist Jimi Hendrix dies, aged 27.
- BOAC flight 775 hijacked by the Popular Front for the Liberation of Palestine.

October
- Huge oil field discovered beneath the North Sea.
- Mark III Ford Cortina goes on sale.

November
- Ten shilling note ceases to be legal tender.
- The first 'Page 3' girl appears in the *Sun*.

December
- The Beatles split up.

PORTSMOUTH In this view of Fratton car sheds on 8 August 1970 are two 4-VEPs, one 4-CEP and Class 933 instruction train S10 on the right, a converted Class 405 unit.

Above: **RICHMOND** Another shed view, this time at Strawberry Hill on 19 May. Ray took this photograph from a moving train, heading for Shepperton at the time.

Right: **CROWTHORNE** EMU No 1037 forms the 10.54 Reading-North Camp special for the 1970 Farnborough Air Show on 13 September. The unit is painted in BR's Intercity blue and grey livery.

Right: **CROWTHORNE** On the previous day, looking from the same vantage point but in the opposite direction, Ray captured Nos 1205 and 1201 forming the 17.24 Guildford-Reading service.

Below: **GUILDFORD** 4-SUB No 4382 was photographed in wintry conditions at Guildford on 3 April. These popular suburban units, which could seat six passengers across, were introduced by the Southern Railway's legendary Chief Mechanical Engineer, Oliver Bulleid, in 1941 and were built at Eastleigh through to 1951. Bulleid was of course best known for his classic steam locomotives, like the magnificent 'Merchant Navy' and 'West Country' Class 'Pacifics', but once steam had been consigned to the history books only his electric legacy remained.

WIMBLEDON PARK Here's another
4-SUB, this time No 4750, at Wimbledon Park.
These trains had a maximum speed of 75mph.

Day of the diesel

CLAPHAM I love this photograph Ray took on 22 November of a Brush Type 4 (later Class 47) coming round the curve off the Western Region at Clapham to join Southern Region rails, with a train of ten Intercity coaches in tow. In the foreground, young footballers are honing their skills – perhaps hoping one day to emulate the 1970 England team, skippered by Bobby Moore, which many pundits said was even better than the 1966 winning squad … but had crashed out of the World Cup in Mexico four months earlier after losing 3-2 to West Germany in extra time in the quarter finals. Sounds familiar, doesn't it?

The Class 47 was probably the most successful of all British Rail's diesel-electric locomotives. It was certainly the most numerous main-line diesel, with a total of 512 built at Crewe and at Brush's Loughborough works between 1962 and 1968. They were powered by Sulzer twin-bank 12-cylinder engines producing 2,750bhp (later in the 1970s de-rated to 2,580bhp), and were capable of 95mph. More than 30 examples have been saved from the scrapyard by enthusiasts and can be seen in action on heritage lines across the country; for example, the Mid Norfolk Railway, which specialises in diesel traction, has two. You can also see a few still in action on the nation's railway network hauling freight and charter trains for enthusiasts.

WATERLOO Here's another classic diesel locomotive – this time 'Warship' No D819 *Goliath* waiting at London Waterloo to head the 15.10 express to Exeter on 19 March. The Type 4 'Warship' Class were later designated Class 42, and 38 were built at Swindon between 1958 and 1961 for British Rail's Western Region, based on a diesel-hydraulic design that had proved successful on the West German Federal Railways. Unfortunately, the non-standard design meant that the Class 42s had a short life; *Goliath* was withdrawn on 3 October 1971 and cut up at Swindon in 1972.

Left: **OXFORD** Two more diesel locomotives are seen at Oxford on 23 May, another Brush Type 4 – No D1675 *Amazon* – and a 'Hymek'. The 'Hymek' (later BR Class 35) reinforced the Western Region's reputation for being quirky in its choice of locomotives, as it was another diesel-hydraulic design. Between 1961 and 1964 101 were built by Beyer Peacock, but again their non-standard design counted against them and the entire class had been withdrawn by 1975.

Below: **READING** Here's another of the Western Region's ill-fated diesel-hydraulic locomotives – BR Class 42 No D1040 *Western Queen* on a Paddington to Paignton express, passing through Reading.

It is sometimes said that British Rail's opposition to diesel-hydraulic locomotives had less to do with standardisation than a general anti-German sentiment that still existed in the country so soon after the end of the Second World War. Although diesel-hydraulic technology had been proven in West Germany, it was not the done thing in the 1950s and '60s to admit that the old enemy was better than Britain at anything!

Either way, the 'Western' Class – so called because they all carried two-word names beginning with 'Western' – went the same way as the 'Warships' and 'Hymeks'. *Western Queen*, which entered service in 1962, was cut up just 14 years later.

Above: **READING** Still at Reading, here's another 'Western' – this time No D1046 *Western Marquis* on 7 November. It, too, entered service in 1962 and was scrapped in 1976.

Below: **FARNHAM** The Southern Region's 'Crompton' diesel-electric locomotives were more successful and long-lived. A total of 98 were built between 1960 and 1962 and many continued in service through to the 1990s. Later to be classified BR Class 33, they were capable of 85mph and worked on passenger and freight services. A total of 26 locomotives survive in preservation, but not No 6526, seen here at Farnham on 9 March.

1970
Arrivals & Departures

Arrivals

Minnie Driver	Actress	31 January
James Purnell	Politician	2 March
Kylie Travis	Actress	27 April
Uma Thurman	Actress	29 April
Andre Agassi	Tennis player	29 April
Louis Theroux	Author	20 May
Naomi Campbell	Model	22 May
Joseph Fiennes	Actor	27 May
Lucy Benjamin	Actress	25 June
Andi Peters	TV presenter	29 July
Alan Shearer	Footballer	13 August
Darren Gough	Cricketer	18 September
Edwin van der Sar	Footballer	29 October
Zoe Ball	TV presenter	23 November
Aled Jones	Singer	29 December

Departures

Bertrand Russell	Philosopher	(b1872)	2 February
Hugh Dowding	RAF Air Chief Marshal	(b1882)	15 February
Gypsy Rose Lee	Striptease artiste	(b1913)	26 April
E. M. Forster	Writer	(b1879)	7 June
Iain Macleod	Politician	(b1913)	20 July
John Barbirolli	Conductor	(b1899)	29 July
Gamal Abdel Nasser	Egyptian President	(b1918)	28 September
Janis Joplin	Rock singer	(b1943)	4 October
Lillian Board	Athlete	(b1948)	26 December
Sonny Liston	Boxer	(b1932)	30 December

Above: **ASCOT** Here's a real rarity – a Class 46 'Peak' Class diesel makes a rare foray from the Midlands to haul a race special to Ascot on 17 June. These locomotives were known as 'Peaks' because the first ten built (Class 44) were named after British mountains. The usually meticulous Ray Ruffell neglected to make a note of which locomotive he had photographed on this occasion, but it appears to be No D162.

The 'Peaks' were built in 1959 and 1960 and started life on the Midland Main Line from St Pancras, but were later assigned to freight duties until withdrawal began in 1980. Two of the original named Class 44s have been preserved, on the Midland Railway and Peak Rail.

Below: **WEST BYFLEET** Finally, here's my favourite – an eight-car 'Blue Pullman' set pictured near West Byfleet on 25 April, on an educational tour to South Wales via Guildford and Reading.

The 'Blue Pullmans' were luxury trains used from 1960 to 1973. They were the first Pullman diesel-electric multiple units and set the scene for the InterCity 125s that followed. There were two versions: two 1st Class six-car sets for the London Midland Region, and three two-class eight-car sets for the Western Region. By the time this photograph was taken, the trains' days were numbered. By 1972, 1st Class accommodation in BR's Mark II coaches had improved to the level where paying a premium for a Pullman seat was no longer a sensible option. In 1973 they were withdrawn and, astonishingly, none were preserved.

The 'Blue Pullman' has a special appeal to me. At the age of eight I woke up on Christmas Day in 1964 to find a large parcel at the foot of the bed. My heart leapt as I unwrapped a Triang 'Blue Pullman' train set. How did Santa know that was exactly what I'd wanted? Oh, happy days...

Talking of the 'Blue Pullmans', my contacts in the model railway world tell me that Bachmann produce an OO gauge model of the six-car set in incredible detail that includes interior lighting – and even illuminated table lamps. It was released at the end of 2012, priced at a shade under £350. Model railways aren't toys any more – this is a hobby dominated by adults. Sadly – to me, at least – the toys we loved back then would find little favour with today's youngsters, who prefer computer games. It's tragic that the amazing models available today aren't being snapped up by eager youngsters.

DMU domination

Diesel multiple units (DMUs) were an essential part of British Rail's strategy to make its quieter branch lines pay. Although the Great Western Railway had introduced diesel-mechanical railcars as early as 1934, it was not until the early 1950s, after nationalisation, that BR embraced the DMU concept.

Steam-operated branch-line railways were hugely expensive in terms of manpower. A driver, fireman and guard employed on a train consisting of a couple of coaches (and sometimes not many more passengers) clearly was never going to pay its way. And that is not taking into account the manpower required to prepare and dispose of steam locos on a daily basis.

Early railcar experiments proved successful, encouraging BR to authorise a large fleet of new DMUs under the controversial 1955 Modernisation Plan. Huge numbers were built between 1956 and 1963, by a variety of British companies (at the insistence of the British Government at the time). This resulted in an astonishing variety of rolling stock, with many of the DMUs incompatible with rolling stock from other manufacturers. Most were diesel-mechanical, but some were diesel-hydraulic. This, of course, largely demolished one of the prime advantages of DMUs – namely that trains could be quickly added to or split according to passenger demand. In other words, it was

a typical British cock-up caused by interference from meddling politicians who knew little about the running of a railway! Some things never change… Yet, against all odds, some of the early units were not only successful, but also reliable and long-lived, surviving in service until the 1980s, when they were replaced by new 'Sprinter' units.

The branch lines in my native East Anglia were a stronghold of the early DMUs. Thus we saw Class 100 (Gloucester Railway Carriage & Wagon Company), Class 101 (Metro-Cammell), Class 105 (Cravens) and Class 108 (Derby Lightweight) DMUs in large numbers. But not for long – the cruel Beeching axe saw most of my local lines (King's Lynn-Hunstanton, King's Lynn-March, King's Lynn-Dereham) disappear in the late 1960s. My other local line, the former Midland & Great Northern Joint, had gone even earlier, in 1959.

But, of course, every region of Britain had its own specialities in this era. Because of the predominance of third-rail EMUs, Ray Ruffell's native Southern Region lines did not boast many DMUs. But on his travels to other parts of Britain, he was eager to wield his camera when one came into view.

PWLLHELI The light, airy feel of the DMUs was popular with passengers. There is standing room only on this service from Machynlleth to Pwllheli, via Barmouth, on 29 May, yet it does not look uncomfortable. Note the young teenager standing at the front of the train, enjoying the panoramic view ahead – something that certainly wasn't possible in a locomotive-hauled train.

Left: **BARMOUTH** And here is the driver's-eye view of the road ahead, as he eases his DMU into Barmouth on the same day. The crowd by the level crossing gates may have to wait a while yet, as another DMU is heading in the opposite direction, towards Machynlleth.

Below left: **LEAMINGTON SPA** Now we're at Leamington Spa station – at the very platforms from which a young trainspotter named Pete Waterman became enthused with a lifelong love of railways – a love so great that once he'd earned a small fortune in the music industry in the 1980s as one-third of the Stock Aiken Waterman hits factory, he spent some of it on briefly being part-owner of the historic *Flying Scotsman* locomotive! Pete, of course, was inspired by the Great Western steam locomotives that thundered through Leamington in the 1950s. I am not sure how enthusiastic he would have been about railcar No M55008 waiting at the platform on 16 November 1970.

It is, however, a bit of a rarity. Only 20 of these Class 122 single-car units were built by the Gloucester Railway Carriage & Wagon Company. They were nicknamed 'Bubble Cars' at the time of their introduction on the London Midland Region in 1958, although it isn't immediately obvious why – they look nothing like the contemporary Messerschmitt road-going 'bubble car' of that era! Although only capable of 70mph from the twin 150bhp diesel-mechanical engines, they proved popular and most stayed in service until the 1980s. This particular railcar was scrapped in 1984, but six of its siblings have survived into preservation on heritage lines – namely on the South Devon, East Lancashire, Gloucestershire Warwickshire, Battlefield, Ecclesbourne Valley and Mid Norfolk railways.

BARMOUTH A two-car Class 101 unit negotiates one of Britain's most picturesque railway lines, at Barmouth on 12 November. Built by Metro-Cammell at Washwood Heath, Birmingham, from 1956 to 1959, the Class 101s were one of the most successful and longest-lived DMUs, the final five units being withdrawn on 24 December 2003. The oldest set was, by then, just over 47 years old. Because the units were so numerous and long-lived, no fewer than 41 cars have been preserved on heritage railways.

PWLLHELI Ray Ruffell captured this DMU at Pwllheli on 29 May. Unusually, he did not record any other details – and I'm no DMU expert – but I reckon it looks very much like the front end of a Class 100, built by the Gloucester Railway Carriage & Wagon Company Ltd from 1956 to 1958. A total of 40 sets were built, some of which remained in service until the late 1980s. If you know better, please let us know…

DMUs were a mainstay of the rural lines of Wales in 1970 – and still are today, for that matter. Certainly, Wales was a favourite destination for Ray Ruffell and his young family and they regularly returned to his favourite haunts around Barmouth.

Cambria calling

Right: **TALERDDIG** Ray leaned out of the window of the 09.40 Euston to Aberystwyth express on 23 May to capture the Sulzer Type 2 diesel locomotive at the head of the train, storming up to Talerdigg summit in Powys. It's a tribute to the locomotive that it achieved the climb – back in steam days most trains required assistance from a banking engine to tackle this infamous 700-foot challenge.

Below: **TYWYN** The up platform at Tywyn is a quiet place on the morning of 27 May. It is a scene that would have changed little in a century.

Right: **TYWYN** This shabby looking, filthy diesel locomotive, photographed at Tywyn on the same day, would appear to be a well-abused workhorse soon fit only for the scrapyard. But appearances can be deceptive, for this Class 24 Sulzer is one of just four of the 151 in its class built between 1958

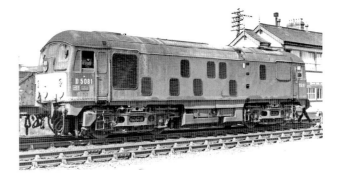

and 1961 to survive in preservation. No D5081 was in fact the final locomotive in its class to be withdrawn from traffic, in 1980, and can now be found delighting enthusiasts on the Gloucestershire Warwickshire heritage railway.

Above: **LLWYNGWRIL**
The small coastal village of Llwyngwril, between Tywyn and Barmouth, was another situated on the former Cambrian Railways coastal line. Its signal box is splendidly ornate on 29 May.

Right: **TAL-Y-BONT** This warning sign dates back to the days when this line was part of the Cambrian Railways, which once owned 230 miles of track. The Cambrian was absorbed by the Great Western Railway in 1922.

Above: **MAWDDACH ESTUARY** Out in the middle of the hauntingly beautiful Mawddach estuary, near Barmouth, are the remains of the Barmouth Junction & Arthog Tramway, which was built by Victorian entrepreneur Solomon Andrews in 1899 as part of his scheme to develop nearby Arthog as a holiday resort. It connected Mawddach to Barmouth Junction, and other lines were built to local quarries to provide building material for the terraces of houses built as part of the holiday resort project. However, the project failed and the tramway was closed in 1903.

BARMOUTH In 1970 a lot of the old railway architecture – much dating back to the Victorian era – was disappearing fast in favour of ugly, modern buildings. With this in mind, Ray was determined to capture as much of the old infrastructure as possible. This is the distinctive frontage of Barmouth Station – note that there isn't a motor vehicle in sight!

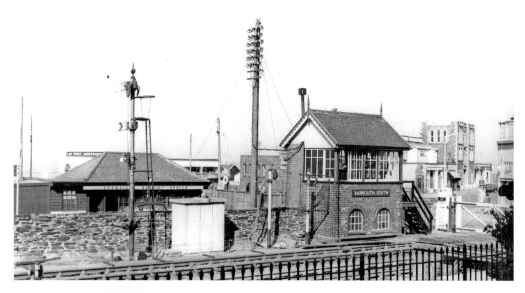

Above: **BARMOUTH**
Barmouth South signal box, signals and level crossing were photographed on 26 May.

Left: **BARMOUTH** This is Barmouth's North box, photographed on the same day.

Right: **BARMOUTH** The North box and the north end of the station are seen from the footbridge. Note the dusting of snow on the tracks – on 26 May!

Above: **BARMOUTH** Ray's wife Joan and their infant daughter Margaret wait for the next DMU at Barmouth on 27 May, bound for Abergynolwyn. It looks like another Class 100, I reckon.

Right: **BARMOUTH** Sadly, there were no steam engine fires to be cleaned here – or anywhere else for that matter – on 2 June 1970.

Far right: **BARMOUTH** On the same day Ray photographed this oddity – a Mini-Track Mobile – by Barmouth South box. It would have been used by track inspection crews.

Above: **HARLECH** A driver's-eye view from a DMU cab, approaching the Harlech up distant signal.

Right: **HARLECH** The 17.01 service from Pwllheli, consisting of a Class 101 DMU, waits for the approaching 16.16 service from Machynlleth to vacate the line ahead on 29 May.

Above: **PENRHYNDEUDRAETH** Another signal box and another DMU at the platform, this time at Penrhyndeudraeth in Gwynedd. The village is close to the mouth of the Afon Dwyryd near Porthmadog, as well as Portmeirion – the latter best known as the filming location for the 1960s TV series *The Prisoner*.

Above right: **CRICCIETH** Here the signal box was also situated on the platform. In the background are the ruins of Criccieth Castle, which overlooks Tremadog Bay. It was built by Llewellyn the Great in the 13th century but was destroyed in the 15th century during a rebellion. Former British Prime Minister David Lloyd George grew up in Criccieth.

Right: **BARMOUTH** Later in the year, on 9 November, the Ruffells were back in Wales. Joan and Margaret are braving the elements on a stormy autumn day, with Barmouth Bridge visible in the distance.

Above: **BARMOUTH** A Metro-Cammell Class 101 DMU makes its way across Barmouth Bridge on the same day.

Left: **BARMOUTH** Another two-car Class 101 Metro-Cammell DMU crosses Barmouth Bridge on 12 November. We are, as ever, eternally grateful to Ray for his sheer determination in seeking out the best possible scenic vantage points to take atmospheric photographs like this glorious study.

Ray managed two trips to the Midlands in 1970, setting off from London Euston on the West Coast Main Line (WCML), which had been the first main line to be electrified following the 1955 Modernisation Plan, completed in stages between 1959 and 1974. The first stretch to be electrified was Crewe to Manchester, completed on 12 September 1960, followed by Crewe to Liverpool, opened on 1 January 1962. Electrification was then extended southwards and the first electric trains from London ran on 12 November 1965, although a full service did not start until 18 April the following year. Electrification of the Birmingham line was completed on 6 March 1967, and in March 1970 the Government gave approval to the electrification of the northern section to Glasgow, which opened on 6 May 1974.

By 1970 a new set of high-speed long-distance services had been introduced, known as the Intercity services and slashing journey times. For example, London to Manchester took 2hr 40min (10 minutes less for the twice-daily 'Manchester Pullman').

Rail enthusiasts and general public alike missed the crack LMS steam expresses that had once raced north from Euston on these lines, but they also appreciated the reduced journey times. Under steam power, the best timing for the London to Glasgow route was 6½ hours, set in the late 1930s by the 'Coronation Scot'. Electrification meant the same journey took 5 hours. No wonder passenger traffic on the West Coast Main Line doubled between 1962 and 1975.

WOLVERHAMPTON Ray's first trip of the year on the WCML was in June. At Wolverhampton on the 6th he photographed No E3065 in a siding at Wolverhampton. It is a member of the 40-strong British Rail Class 85 – one of five prototype classes built and evaluated in the early 1960s that eventually led to the development of the Class 86 locomotive. All were built between 1961 and 1964 by BR at Doncaster Works to haul trains from Birmingham to Crewe, Manchester, Liverpool and Preston, prior to the electrification to London. All 40 of the 3,200bhp Class 85s had been withdrawn by 1991; only one survived into preservation, and is currently being restored at Barrow Hill Engine Shed by the AC Locomotive Group. The rest were scrapped at MC Metals, Glasgow.

Above: **WOLVERHAMPTON** It wasn't all electric on the WCML. On the same day Ray photographed Class 25 D7558, probably on freight duties. A total of 327 of these popular BR Type 2 locos were built between 1961 and 1967 at Crewe, Darlington and Derby. With a power output of 1,250bhp and generating 39,000lb/ft of tractive effort (torque), these were primarily designed as freight workhorses but, with a top speed of 90mph, those fitted with heating boilers were also pressed into service on passenger duties. The final Class 25 was withdrawn from service in 1987, although 20 have survived in preservation on heritage lines across the country.

Above right: **BIRMINGHAM NEW STREET** Another diesel, Brush Type 4 (later Class 47) No 1623, is newly arrived at the head of an Intercity express from Southampton.

Right: **WOLVERHAMPTON** Ray returned to the Midlands in the autumn. This is Wolverhampton on 7 November, with Class 119 DMU No M51102, another product of the Gloucester Railway Carriage & Wagon Company, showing Shrewsbury on its destination blind

Above: **WOLVERHAMPTON** Standing in the station on the same day are a couple of Metro-Cammell three-car DMUS.

Left: **SHREWSBURY** Severn Bridge Junction, just south of Shrewsbury station, was a busy place in 1970. It was controlled by the impressive Severn Bridge Junction signal box, built in 1903 and opened in 1904; today it is the largest surviving mechanical signal box in the world, boasting a 180-lever frame. At the time of writing in 2012 it is a listed building, operates 24 hours a day, is permanently manned by two signalmen, and is expected to remain in service until at least 2030, according to Network Rail.

BIRMINGHAM Freight and the way it was transported was changing fast in 1970, with the advent of the container. Birmingham Inland Port was set up by British Rail to deal with customs clearances for exports and imports, with containers unloaded from trains for onward transport by road. But it was not long before companies began to cut out the 'middleman' – the railway – and simply use cheaper road hauliers to pick up the containers from Britain's ports.

Southern landmarks

Many rail enthusiasts of the era were so besotted with trains that they were virtually blinkered to the railway infrastructure around them, and did not realise that the everyday buildings and paraphernalia of Britain's railways were every bit as important as the locomotives and rolling stock.

Not so Ray Ruffell! Ray was a 'big picture' man. He was aware that railway buildings as important as Euston's legendary Doric Arch had been demolished in the name of progress in the 1960s, and was determined to record what was left of our Victorian legacy, as well as the modern monstrosities that were replacing it at an alarming rate by 1970.

In 2012 it is hard to believe that the jewel in the crown of London's great stations – St Pancras – had been under threat of demolition as recently as 1966. Fortunately, public opinion had been roused by the demolition of the Euston Arch, and the railway-loving Sir John Betjeman, then Poet Laureate, took up the cause to protect the station, which, when completed in 1868, had been the largest enclosed space in the world. In 1967 St Pancras was finally awarded Grade 1 listing. Thank heavens it was saved! Today,

following an £800 million restoration and modernisation programme, St Pancras International is again an iconic landmark station – where you can catch a train direct to Paris, eat in a world-class restaurant, shop in a fresh food market and drink in an award-winning-gastro pub.

So, without further ado, let's look at the railway scene in 1970.

Above right: **CAMBERLEY** This is the timeless scene at Camberley station on the morning of 5 November. The station sign and lights may have changed – and no doubt the bicycles in the corrugated bike shed are a little more modern – but otherwise little would have changed from the Victorian era.

Right: **SURBITON** A contrasting architectural style is seen at Surbiton on 7 May, where a 12-car express from Portsmouth Harbour to Waterloo is passing through. The Southern Railway completely rebuilt the original 1845 station in 1939, with two island platforms. The buildings were designed by architect J. Robb Scott in an art deco style.

Just over a year after this photograph was taken, a major incident occurred at this spot. On 4 July 1971 a freight train

derailed on the points at the London end of Platforms 3 and 4, and two derailed wagons toppled over, obstructing the down fast through line. Moments later, a down passenger express collided with the derailed wagons at speed, causing the front of the train to derail and fall over. Fortunately there were no fatalities.

Above: **DORKING** This is Dorking North station on 13 May, with an assortment of EMUs at the platform and in the sidings. Savour this image, for the unspoiled Victoriana of Dorking North was demolished in 1980 to make way for a very ordinary red-brick replacement, which included a three-storey office block.

Incidentally, Dorking North has now been renamed simply Dorking, despite the fact that it is one of three stations that serve the town. The others are Dorking West and Dorking Deepdene.

Above: **LEATHERHEAD** Still in Surrey, here's a redundant railway building that on 19 March 1970 was enjoying a new lease of life as a motor garage. It is an ex-London, Brighton & South Coast Railway engine shed, which Ray snapped from a passing train.

Above right: **ASH** The former loco shed at Ash is in good repair and, presumably, being used as a storage facility when this photograph was taken, on 17 June. Incidentally, if you happen to be a motoring enthusiast, you will probably know that this

was the day when the original Range Rover was launched, 200 miles away in Cornwall. It was also the last day of Harold Wilson's first term as Prime Minister. On the 18th Edward Heath's Conservatives swept to victory in the General Election.

Right: **PORTSMOUTH** 'Is this the shortest industrial railway in the world?' writes Ray, rhetorically, on the back of this photograph, which he took at Farlington Junction, near Portsmouth, on 8 August. You can see where he's coming from…

Above: **CROWTHORNE** station, Berkshire, opened in 1859 as a result of pressure on the directors of the South Eastern Railway from the governors of nearby Wellington College, who actually contributed £500 towards the cost of building the halt. As a result, the station was originally named 'Wellington College for Crowthorne' until 1928, when it was renamed simply Crowthorne. This is a view of Platform 1 (the up side) on 13 September.

Below: **CROWTHORNE** And this is the scene the same day on Platform 2 (the down side). The horrible bus-stop-style shelter was erected after 1967, when the station was de-staffed and the old buildings fell into disrepair. Happily, the run-down station was enhanced in the mid-1980s, when the glass monstrosity was replaced by a new brick-built shelter.

Above: **BAGSHOT** On 5 November Bagshot station boasted a fine footbridge, ornate platform canopies, and a footway across the tracks made from old sleepers, across which a railway worker is wheeling his pushbike.

Below: **ASH** Ray is travelling on ex-Guildford 4-COR EMU No 3131 through a wintry wonderland as it passes Ash Vale Junction signal box en route to Waterloo, via Ascot.

Above: **WIMBLEDON** These are the Durnsford Road Repair Shops at Wimbledon on 18 March, with a mixture of EMUs in for servicing.

Left: **HOLMWOOD** station serves the nearby villages of Beare Green and South Holmwood, in Surrey. On 13 May the distinctive platform signal box was still manned. Today it is disused, but still in situ.

Farnborough Air Show

The Farnborough International Air Show is a seven-day international trade fair for the aerospace industry, and is held in even-numbered years at Farnborough Airport, Hampshire (the Paris Air Show is held in the odd-numbered years).

Today it is an important event for the aerospace industry, known particularly for the announcement of new developments and orders, but in the 1950s and '60s – when the British aircraft industry led the world in the design of modern jet aircraft – it was a huge draw for the general public, who attended in tens of thousands. Even in 1970 special excursions were laid on from all over the country, bringing visitors to the show.

While the show visitors were marvelling at the latest aeronautic developments, our photographer Ray Ruffell would be at the side of the local tracks, capturing the trains heading for the event.

SANDHURST One of Ray's favourite vantage points was Sandhurst Cutting, where on Sunday 13 September he captured EMU No 1037 as special empty stock from North Camp to Reading.

Above: **CROWTHORNE** Brush Type 4 (Class 47) diesel No 1628 hauls the 08.57 special from Wolverhampton to North Camp, pictured near Crowthorne. Note the mix of blue and grey and the old BR maroon carriages.

Right: **CROWTHORNE** Two three-car DMUs from the Western Region comprise the 18.10 special from North Camp to Reading, entering Crowthorne.

SANDHURST
A classic study of another special, this time 'Hastings' diesel-electric multiple unit No 1035 forming the 10.25 Guildford-Reading service between Sandhurst and Crowthorne.

CROWTHORNE
Another pair of three-car DMUs from the Western Region heads for Reading.

Freight

Left: **BARMOUTH** The locomotive at the head of this mixed freight train approaching Barmouth on 9 November is Class 24 No 5080. In all, 151 Class 24s were built at British Railways' Derby, Darlington and Crewe works between 1958 and 1961. They were powered by Sulzer six-cylinder diesel engines, producing 1,160bhp but with a top speed of just 75mph. They were all withdrawn by 1980.

Below: **BARMOUTH** At the same location on 28 May is another Class 24, this time No 5041, hauling the daily Pwllheli-Shrewsbury freight.

By 1970 freight transport was in transition. Shipping had been transformed by the introduction of containers and, although these figured on the railways too, on British Rail most freight was still carried in wagons that had changed little in a hundred years.

Left: **CLAPHAM** For sheer pulling power it was difficult to beat a Brush Type 4, and here's one on 11 January near Clapham Junction hauling a gleaming train of new 100-ton cement wagons. Ray snapped this photo from the rear of the 12.28 Waterloo-Reading EMU.

Below: **GUILDFORD** On 14 January Class 37 No D6961 heads an oil train from Thames Haven to North Camp. Between 1960 and 1965 399 of these versatile Type 3 mixed-traffic locomotives were built by English Electric at the Vulcan Foundry and by Robert Stephenson & Hawthorns; rated at 1,750bhp, they were capable of 90mph. Remarkably, some of the class remain in service in 2012, despite being half a century old, while several have been preserved on heritage railways.

Below: **ASCOT** Heading this oil train from Thames Haven to Earley is No E6001, the first of the unusual Class 73 electro-diesel locomotives. Forty-nine of these remarkable machines were built between 1962 and 1967 at Eastleigh and the Vulcan Foundry – remarkable because they could operate from the Southern Region's 650/750V DC third rail or from an onboard diesel engine that allowed them to operate on non-electrified routes. On paper this made these locos very versatile, although in reality the diesel engine produced less power than was available from the third-rail supply, so the locomotives rarely strayed from Southern rails. Several of the class are still working, including one that now belongs to Eurostar. Those that have been withdrawn are popular on heritage railways, as the small diesel engine is more than capable of hauling trains at the regulation top speed of 25mph. Among those preserved is No E6001 itself, which can be seen in operation on the Dean Forest Railway.

Right: **CLAPHAM** The powerful Class 45 diesel locomotives were built between 1959 and 1960 to haul expresses on the Midland Main Line between St Pancras and Manchester, replacing redundant steam locos. However, by 1970 many were reduced to freight duties – like No D73, pictured at Clapham on 16 March, hauling a coal train from the Midlands to Kent.

Right: **CLAPHAM** Another former passenger express locomotive that had fallen on hard times was 'Western' No 1025 *Western Guardsman*, pictured at Clapham Junction with a mixed freight from Severn Tunnel Junction to Norwood.

Below right: **WOKING** At first glance this is an ordinary 1970 scene at Woking, with 350bhp diesel shunter No D4103 at work in the sidings. But look closely and you will see an ex-Great Western Railway 'Toad' brake van behind the engine – the name was derived from the GWR's telegraphic code for such a vehicle. The standard GWR brake van design dated from 1894, and many varieties were built between 1894 and 1948. Early vans weighed 10 or 12 tons, but this gradually increased to 20 tons. Each 'Toad' had a large guard's cabin extending about two-thirds of the length of the van, with the remaining third open at the sides but covered with a roof. Full-length external footboards and hand rails allowed the guard or shunter to ride on the outside during shunting movements.

Assorted wagons

We've already looked at the changing nature of freight rolling stock on British Railways in 1970. There really was an astonishing assortment of wagons in those days and there now follow a few snapshots Ray took of some that he spotted on his travels during the year.

WOKING This 25-ton engineers' brake van, spotted in a siding at Woking on 4 May, dates back to 1926.

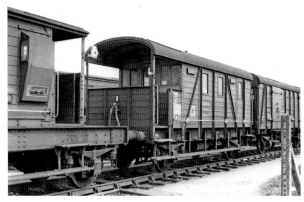

WOKING Also at Woking on the same day is an ex-SR 'Vanfit', fitted with the vacuum brake for fast running but now assigned to engineering duties.

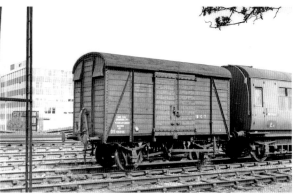

1970 No 1 Records

January
Two Little Boys	Rolf Harris
Love Grows (Where My Rosemary Goes)	Edison Lighthouse

February
Wand'rin Star	Lee Marvin

March
Bridge Over Troubled Water	Simon & Garfunkel

April
All Kinds of Everything	Dana

May
Spirit in the Sky	Norman Greenbaum
Back Home	England World Cup Squad

June
Yellow River	Christie
In the Summertime	Mungo Jerry

August
The Wonder of You	Elvis Presley

September
Tears of a Clown	Smokey Robinson and the Miracles
Band of Gold	Freda Payne

October
Woodstock	Matthews Southern Comfort

November
Voodoo Child (Slight Return)	Jimi Hendrix Experience
I Hear You Knocking	Dave Edmunds' Rockpile

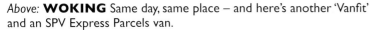

Above: **WOKING** Same day, same place – and here's another 'Vanfit' and an SPV Express Parcels van.

Above right: **WOKING** Ray was busy on 4 May at Woking! This time he has captured three 'fishy' wagons in the siding. No, they didn't transport fish – they were actually ballast wagons. From the earliest days of Britain's railways, train companies applied names to their rolling stock in the form of codes to simplify describing them by telegraph. Hence 24-ton three-way ballast hoppers like that in the centre were known as 'Dogfish', and this example is flanked on either end by 17-ton ballast hoppers known as 'Mackerel'. It's a shame there isn't a track-laying flat wagon with a crane – that was known as a 'Salmon'.

Right: **BARMOUTH** Standard gauge steam locomotives had long departed British Rail by 26 May 1970, but traces of the former motive power remained if you looked closely enough. Eagle-eyed Ray spotted this former ex-ROD 2-8-0 tender in a siding at the north end of Barmouth station.

All in a day's work

GUILDFORD Whoops! Were the icy conditions on 4 February responsible for No D6581 going off the road and piling into this bridge abutment at Guildford?

GUILDFORD Who said steam power was dead? On 1 November this Aveling Porter road roller turned up at Guildford station forecourt for a top-up of water, which staff were happy to supply.

PECKHAM Finally, here's a rare photograph of our photographer, Ray Ruffell (standing), on duty as fellow staff attach electro-diesel No E6042 to 4-SUB EMU No 4621 at Queens Road, Peckham, when for some reason the 'juice' had been turned off. We're not sure who picked up Ray's camera to take a snap of the maestro himself, but I'm sure you'll agree it is good to see the man behind the lens who provided us with such a thorough insight into the changing world of Britain's railways in 1970. Thanks, Ray!

Index

Acknowledgements

Many thanks to the family of the late Ray Ruffell, without whose efforts to photograph and record the changing railway scene in 1970 this book would not have been possible.